Stump the Ump
The question and answer book on the
rules of baseball.

By
Richard Kent

Illustrated by Mike Dywelska

Stump the Ump
The question and answer book on the rules of baseball.

Published by Funsport Publications Inc.

I.S.B.N. :0-9693804-0-2

Typesetting by Gandalf Typographers, Toronto
Printed by Maracle Press Limited

Printed in Canada

To Ron Kent

Men on first and second, one out. Batter spanks double to left, runner from second scores, runner from first thrown out at plate. Batter-runner stands at second but missed first base on the way. Defensive team makes appeal at first. What is the call at first; does the run count?

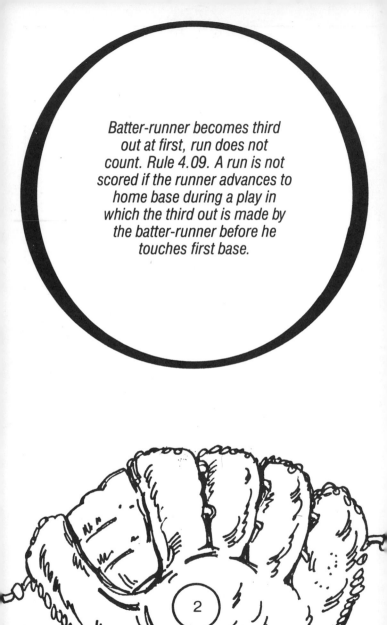

Batter-runner becomes third out at first, run does not count. Rule 4.09. A run is not scored if the runner advances to home base during a play in which the third out is made by the batter-runner before he touches first base.

2

Runner caught in wild run-down between third and home. Exhausted runner makes it back to third base only to discover runner from second standing on bag. Shortstop tags both runners occupying third. Double play?

3

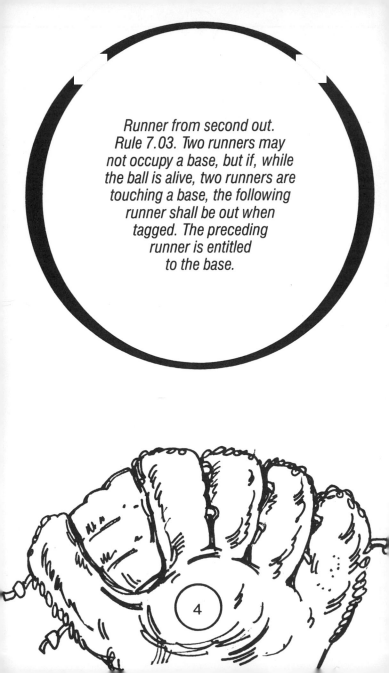

*Runner from second out.
Rule 7.03. Two runners may
not occupy a base, but if, while
the ball is alive, two runners are
touching a base, the following
runner shall be out when
tagged. The preceding
runner is entitled
to the base.*

4

Nobody out, man on third. Wind pushed pop-up puts catcher in opposition dugout. Roaming around rivals backstop fields foul then falls on face. Rapid runner heads home but perfect peg to pitcher puts player out at plate. Double play?

Batter's out, runner scores. Rule 7.04. A fielder or catcher may reach or step into, or go into the dugout with one or both feet to make catch, and if he holds the ball, the catch shall be allowed. Ball is in play. If the fielder or catcher should fall while in the dugout after making a legal catch, the ball is dead and runners advance one base without liability to be put out.

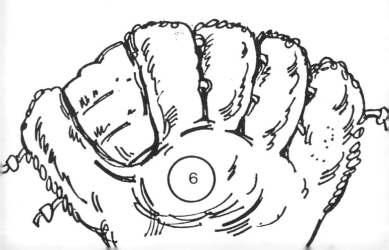

6

Men on first and second, one out. Pop-up to second baseman. Umpire immediately declares "Infield Fly."
Is the batter out, may runners advance?

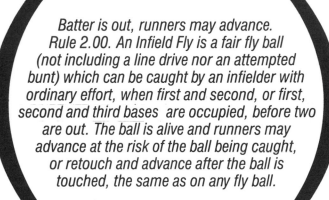

Batter is out, runners may advance.
Rule 2.00. An Infield Fly is a fair fly ball
(not including a line drive nor an attempted
bunt) which can be caught by an infielder with
ordinary effort, when first and second, or first,
second and third bases are occupied, before two
are out. The ball is alive and runners may
advance at the risk of the ball being caught,
or retouch and advance after the ball is
touched, the same as on any fly ball.

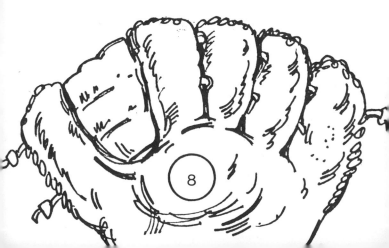

8

Cleanup hitter clubs monster triple. Opposition manager requests measurement of monster club. Bat is 42″ long, 2 1/2″ in diameter at the fattest part, pine-tarred and taped along the handle for a foot and a half from its end. Legal lumber?

9

Legal. Rule 1.10 The bat shall be not more than 2 3/4 inches in diameter at the thickest part and not more than 18 inches from its end, may be covered or treated with any material or substance to improve the grip.

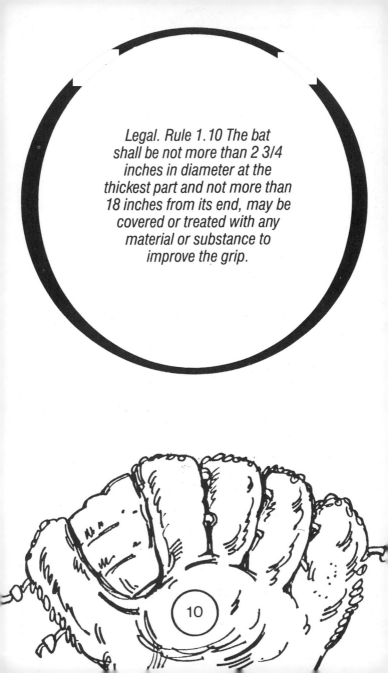

10

Man on second, two out. Batter rips a shot up the middle. Scorched ball hits edge of second base on the fly and ricochets in the air, untouched, onto foul ground. Man from second scores, batter-runner stands on first. Fair or foul ball?

*Fair ball. Rule 2.00. A fair
ball is a batted ball that touches
first, second or third base.*

Opening day madness; rowdy fans invade the field. Visiting manager asks umpire-in-chief for forfeit. During discussion, one smoke bomb and two streakers land in left field. Disgusted manager pulls visitors from the field.
Has home team forfeited game?

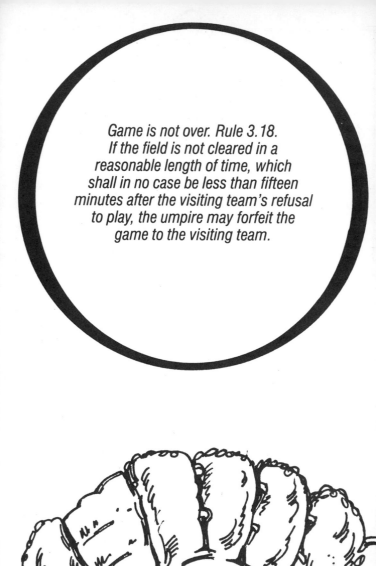

*Game is not over. Rule 3.18.
If the field is not cleared in a
reasonable length of time, which
shall in no case be less than fifteen
minutes after the visiting team's refusal
to play, the umpire may forfeit the
game to the visiting team.*

14

Blistering blast to deep left-centre; left fielder races into gap. Making valiant valid effort to spear liner, big leaguer loses leather. Flying glove knocks down sure triple holding batter to a single.
What is the call?

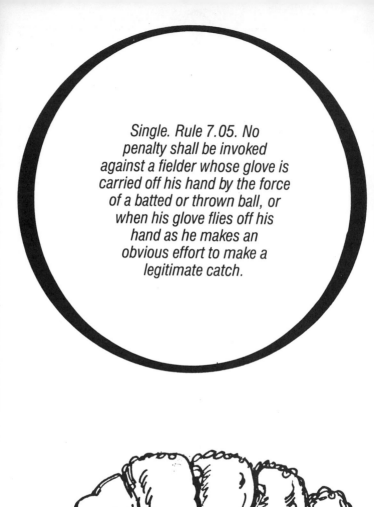

Single. Rule 7.05. No penalty shall be invoked against a fielder whose glove is carried off his hand by the force of a batted or thrown ball, or when his glove flies off his hand as he makes an obvious effort to make a legitimate catch.

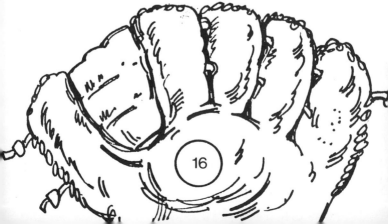

16

Bases loaded, none out. Hard hit grounder to first baseman. First baseman fields ball and steps on first before batter-runner gets to base. Strong throw to the shortstop standing on second beats runner from first and shortstop's throw to third baseman standing on third beats runner from second. Triple play?

One out. Batter-runner out at first, runners from first and second safe, must be tagged out. Rule 2.00. A force play is a play in which a runner legally loses his right to occupy a base by reason of the batter becoming a runner.

(Batter never became a runner; therefore, runners from first and second were not forced to reach next base and had to be tagged out).

Man on first, one out. Hot shot one hopper to first baseman. Runner on first never makes a move towards second, but runs back and stands on first base. First baseman trots over and tags runner standing on first base and then touches first base. Double Play?

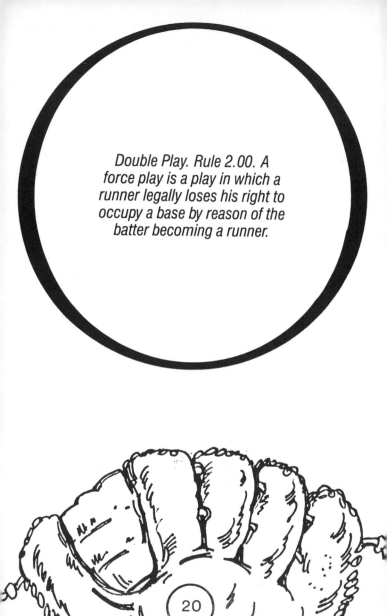

Double Play. Rule 2.00. A force play is a play in which a runner legally loses his right to occupy a base by reason of the batter becoming a runner.

20

April showers bring May doubleheaders.
Cold, wet day keeps everyone away.
Under the stands, two managers and the
umpiring crew discuss whether a single
day game should be started.
Who makes the call?

21

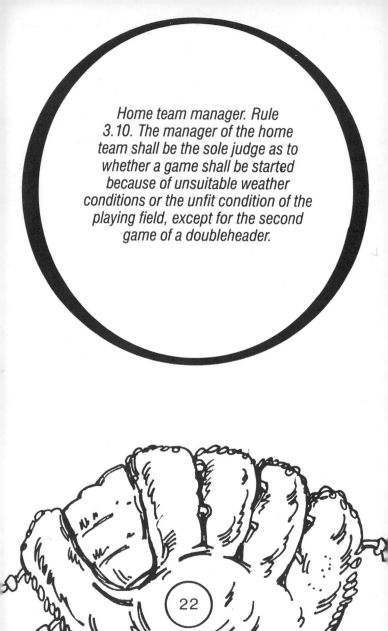

Home team manager. Rule 3.10. The manager of the home team shall be the sole judge as to whether a game shall be started because of unsuitable weather conditions or the unfit condition of the playing field, except for the second game of a doubleheader.

Bottom of the eighth, tie game, bases
loaded, two out. Batter chops high hopper
to second baseman. Batter-runner flies down the
line and is called safe on bang bang play
at first. Visiting manager disagrees with
call, vehemently. Road skipper all over, up
and down men in blue, vein popping
madman finally protests game while
being escorted from field by charges.
Is protest valid?

23

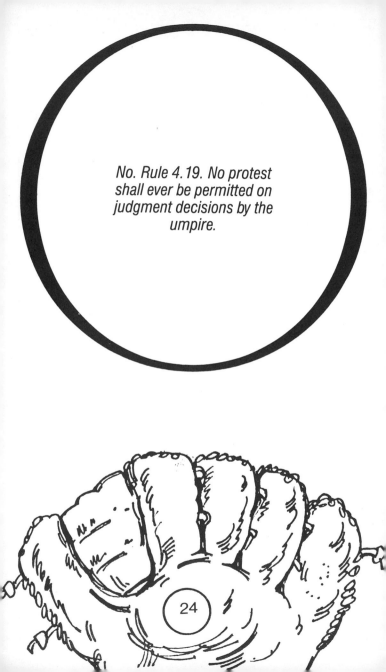

No. Rule 4.19. No protest shall ever be permitted on judgment decisions by the umpire.

Batter pops up by defensive team's dugout, catcher races over to top step. Teetering on edge of stairs, catcher's own player holds him up as he makes great catch. What is the call?

25

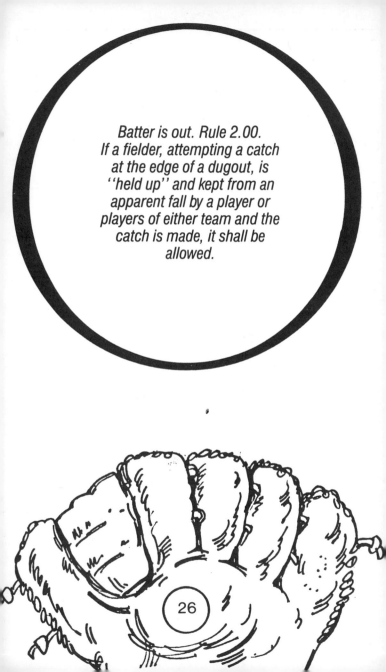

Batter is out. Rule 2.00.
If a fielder, attempting a catch at the edge of a dugout, is ''held up'' and kept from an apparent fall by a player or players of either team and the catch is made, it shall be allowed.

26

Nobody on, nobody out. Speedster lays one fair down third baseline. Pitcher and third baseman break late and have no play at first. Bunt rolling perilously close to foul territory. Suddenly third baseman and pitcher down on their hands and knees. Not touching the ball, boys huff and puff and blow the ball foul. What is the call?

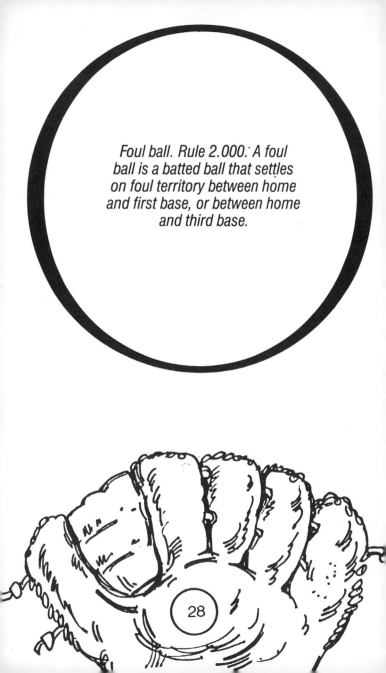

Foul ball. Rule 2.000. A foul ball is a batted ball that settles on foul territory between home and first base, or between home and third base.

Man on second, two out. Line drive to shortstop. Runner breaks for third. Ball deflects off of shortstop's glove down onto sprinting base runner's foot. Without touching the ground, ball kicked by runner thirty feet in the air. Third baseman catches deflected ball and throws to second baseman tagging second. Runner from second stands on third, batter-runner stands on first. What is the call?

No catch, everybody is safe. Rule 2.00. It is not a catch if a fielder touches a fly ball which then hits a member of the offensive team or an umpire and then is caught by another defensive player.

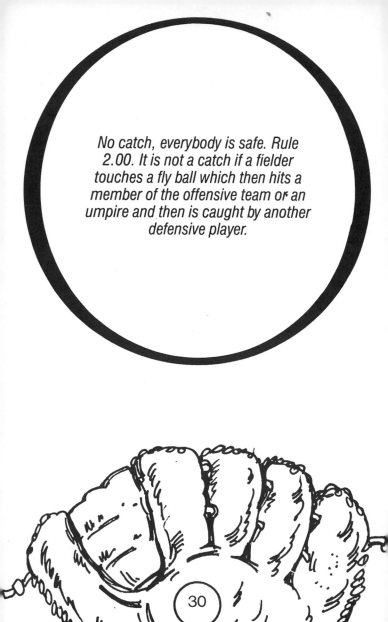

30

Bottom of the ninth, tie game, bases loaded, two out. Left handed pull hitter at the plate. Except for the battery, manager moves entire defensive team onto fair ground on the right side of the diamond. Legal or illegal defense?

Legal. Rule 4.03. Except for the pitcher and the catcher, any fielder may station himself anywhere in fair territory.

32

Bases loaded, batter powers
change-up down the left field line, fair.
Fielder races back to the wall, leaps and
reaches into the seats to catch ball amidst
fans. With player dangling dangerously
over fence, fan rips ball from outfielder's
glove. Peeved player lands back in left
field minus ball. What is the call?

*Grand slam home run.
Rule 2.00. No interference
should be allowed when a
fielder reaches over a fence,
railing, rope or into a stand
to catch a ball. He does so
at his own risk.*

Nobody out, 0-2 count. Pitcher comes in with waist high curve ball. Batter swings and misses but hard biting breaking ball busts way inside and belts batter in...leg. What is the call?

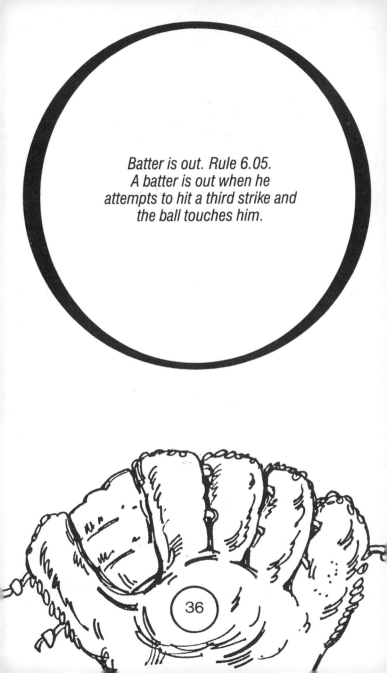

Batter is out. Rule 6.05.
A batter is out when he
attempts to hit a third strike and
the ball touches him.

36

Men on first and second, none out. Sky high pop-up to short. Umpire immediately declares "Infield Fly". Ball is up there a mile drifting into shallow left. Left fielder calls off shortstop, settles under fly ball, drops it, and then boots it. Runners advance one base, batter stands on first. What is the call?

Batter is out. Runners may advance. Rule 2.00. On the infield fly rule the umpire is to rule whether the ball could ordinarily have been handled by an infielder – not by some arbitrary limitations such as the grass or base lines. The umpire must rule also that a ball is an infield fly, even if handled by an outfielder, if, in the umpire's judgment, the ball could have been as easily handled by an infielder. When an infield fly rule is called, runners may advance at their own risk.

Nobody on, nobody out, 1-1 count. Slow working pitcher gets ball from catcher. Hurler steps off mound and adjusts cap and uniform, uses rosin bag, chats with rosin bag, rubs up ball, talks to ball, readjusts cap and uniform. Ritual takes thirty seconds. What is the call?

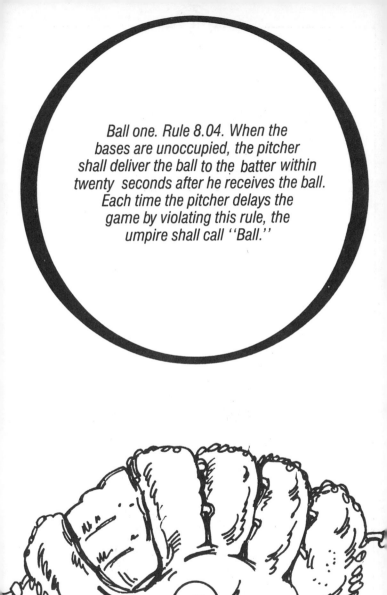

Ball one. Rule 8.04. When the bases are unoccupied, the pitcher shall deliver the ball to the batter within twenty seconds after he receives the ball. Each time the pitcher delays the game by violating this rule, the umpire shall call ''Ball.''

40

Ninety-eight degree August afternoon. Bottom of the sixteenth, tie game, bases loaded, two out. Pitcher gets sign, gets set. Drained, used and abused catcher seeing stars; hard boiled backstop suddenly packs it in, keels over and takes batter down with him. Catcher's interference, balk or no play?

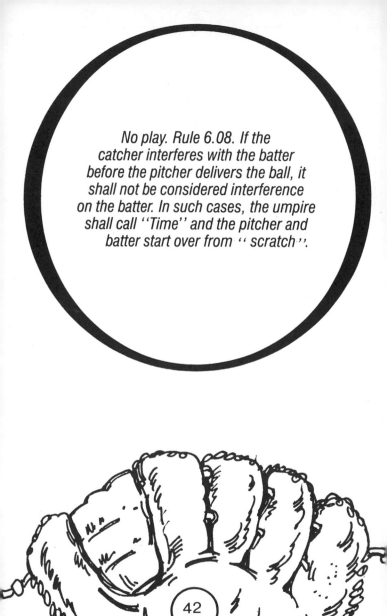

No play. Rule 6.08. If the catcher interferes with the batter before the pitcher delivers the ball, it shall not be considered interference on the batter. In such cases, the umpire shall call "Time" and the pitcher and batter start over from " scratch".

42

Dancing, doctored knuckleball in for
strike. Skeptical umpire examines ball and
finds it to be slippery when wet.
What is the call?

43

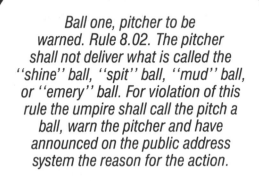

Ball one, pitcher to be warned. Rule 8.02. The pitcher shall not deliver what is called the ''shine'' ball, ''spit'' ball, ''mud'' ball, or ''emery'' ball. For violation of this rule the umpire shall call the pitch a ball, warn the pitcher and have announced on the public address system the reason for the action.

44

One out, 3-0 count.
Batter is batting out of turn.
Defensive team makes appeal.
What is the call?

45

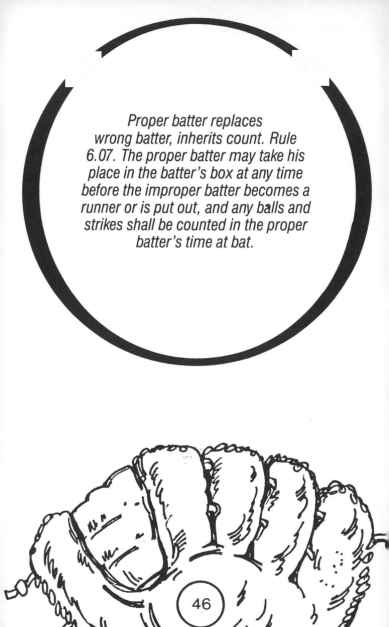

Proper batter replaces wrong batter, inherits count. Rule 6.07. The proper batter may take his place in the batter's box at any time before the improper batter becomes a runner or is put out, and any balls and strikes shall be counted in the proper batter's time at bat.

46

Man on third, one out. Batter drills hanging curve down left field line. In cozy confines of ancient park spectators right on top of play. 330 feet from plate, fan reaches out of stands into foul territory and deflects easily caught fly ball away from left fielder. What is the call?

Batter is out, runner scores from third. Rule 3.16. If spectator interference clearly prevents a fielder from catching a fly ball, the umpire shall declare the batter out. Ball is dead at the time of the call. Because of the distance the ball was hit, the runner on third base would have scored after the catch if the fielder had caught the ball which was interfered with, the runner is permitted to score.

48

Bases loaded, two out, full count.
Knuckleballing pitcher fans
knuckleheaded hitter with pitch in dirt.
Bouncing ball gets by catcher and deflects
off of umpire on way to backstop.
Runners from second and third score,
batter-runner stands on first.
What is the call?

Play counts. Rule 5.09. If a third strike (not a foul tip) passes the catcher and hits an umpire, the ball is in play.

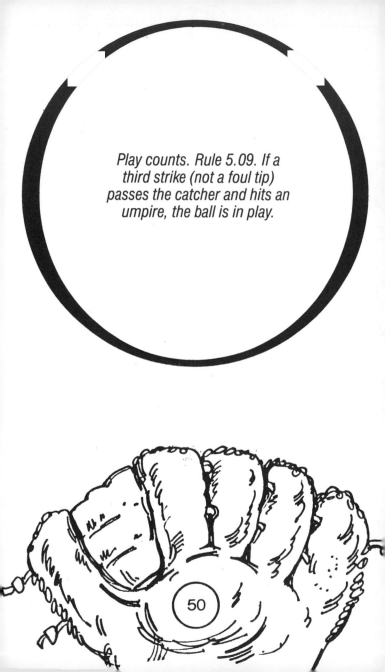

50

Batter hits long looping ground rule double. Standing on second base, batter-runner knows he missed first base so takes opportunity of dead ball to run back and touch first. With dead ball suspension of play in effect, and fans and defensive team going crazy, batter-runner then trots back to second base. When play resumes, defensive team immediately appeals play at first. What is the call?

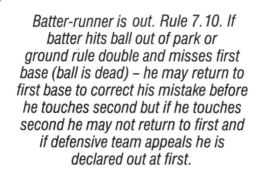

Batter-runner is out. Rule 7.10. If batter hits ball out of park or ground rule double and misses first base (ball is dead) – he may return to first base to correct his mistake before he touches second but if he touches second he may not return to first and if defensive team appeals he is declared out at first.

Men on first and second, one out. Poor pitcher being bombed, booed and tattooed. Rattled righty attempts to pick off runner at first, balks, and throws pitch into right field. On balk runner from second scores and runner from first goes all the way to third. Legal advance?

Legal advance. Rule 8.05. In cases where a pitcher balks and throws wild, either to a base or to home plate, a runner or runners may advance beyond the base to which he is entitled at his own risk.

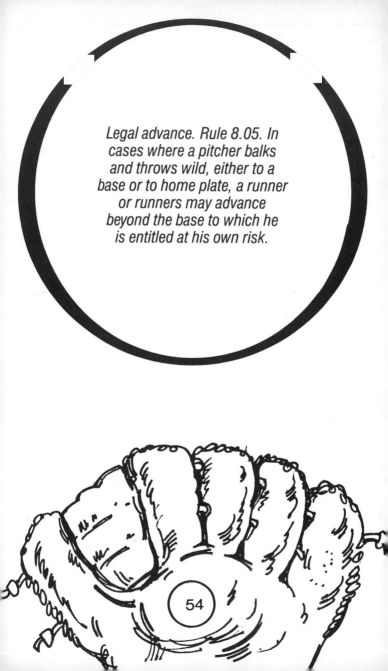

Bottom of the ninth, tie game, nobody on, two out. Cleanup hitter crushes fastball into upper deck. Frenzied fans storm the field. Rounding third base, local hero running for his life abandons base path and sprints into dugout without touching home. Perplexed supporters cancel celebrations. What is the call?

55

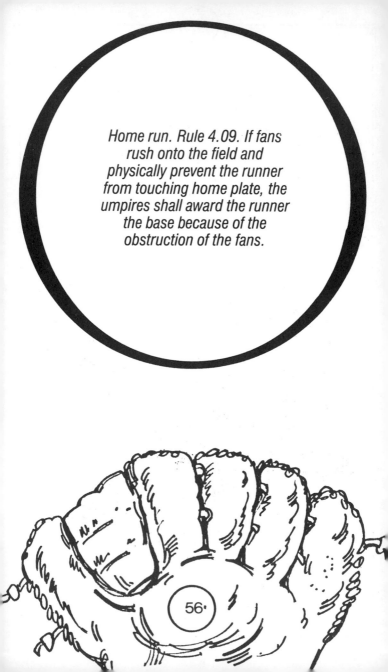

Home run. Rule 4.09. If fans rush onto the field and physically prevent the runner from touching home plate, the umpires shall award the runner the base because of the obstruction of the fans.

Nobody on, nobody out. Wicked line drive down first baseline deflects off   first baseman's glove and hits umpire in head. Ball deflects twenty feet in the air and is caught by first baseman in fair territory in shallow right.
Batter-runner stands on first.
What is the call?

Batter-runner safe at first. Rule 5.09. If a batted ball is deflected by a fielder in fair territory and hits a runner or an umpire while still in flight and then is caught by an infielder it shall not be a catch, but the ball shall remain in play.

Bases loaded, two out. Booming shot ripped down third baseline booted by third baseman. Third sacker recovers ball in time to hang up runner between second and third. Runner from third scores easily before runner from second tagged out. Does the run count?

Run does not count. Rule 4.09. A run is not scored if the runner advances to home base during a play in which the third out is made by any runner being forced out.

Left-handed pull hitter booms blast down
right field line, hooking shot grazes
outside of foul pole and lands in foul
ground. What is the call?

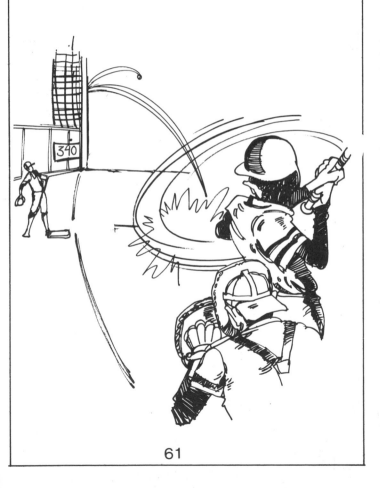

61

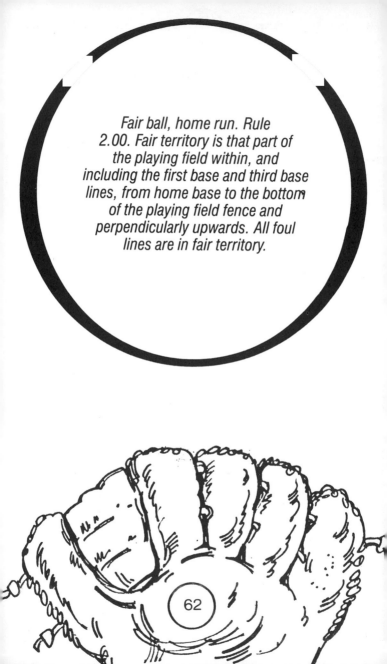

Fair ball, home run. Rule 2.00. Fair territory is that part of the playing field within, and including the first base and third base lines, from home base to the bottom of the playing field fence and perpendicularly upwards. All foul lines are in fair territory.

62

Man on third, one out. Fly ball to right. Sly, slow runner stands ten feet behind base and takes flying start towards home before ball is caught. When ball is caught runner has contact with third base and goes on to score easily. Defensive team appeals play. What is the call?

Runner is out. Rule 7.10. Any runner shall be called out, on appeal, when after a fly ball is caught, he fails to retouch his original base before he or his original base is tagged. "Retouch," in this rule, means to tag up and start from a contact with the base after the ball is caught. A runner is not permitted to take a flying start from a position in back of his base.

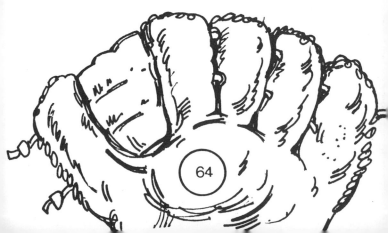

64

Windy, windy day. Bases loaded, one out. Batter uppercuts major league pop-up down the third baseline. Umpire immediately declares ''Infield fly, if fair.'' In shallow left field shortstop and third baseman circle under wind blown ball. Fielders collide, fly ball bounces out of third baseman's glove in fair ground and rolls away in foul territory. All runners advance one base. Batter stands on first. What is the call?

*Batter's out, runners may
advance. Rule 2.00. An Infield Fly is
a fair fly ball which can be caught by an
infielder with ordinary effort, when first and
second, or first, second and third bases are
occupied, before two are out. When it seems
apparent that a batted ball will be an Infield Fly,
the umpire shall immediately declare ''Infield
Fly'' for the benefit of the runners. If the ball is
near the baselines, the umpire shall declare
''Infield Fly, if Fair.'' When an infield Fly
rule is called, runners may advance
at their own risk.*

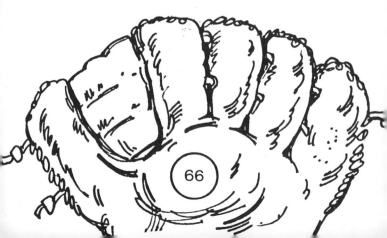

Man on first, one out. Batter lays one
down fair, up the first baseline. Catcher
and batter-runner break for first base. Catcher
and batter-runner collide thirty feet up line.
Catcher and batter-runner roll in dirt beside ball.
Catcher tags batter-runner with fair ball.
What is the call?

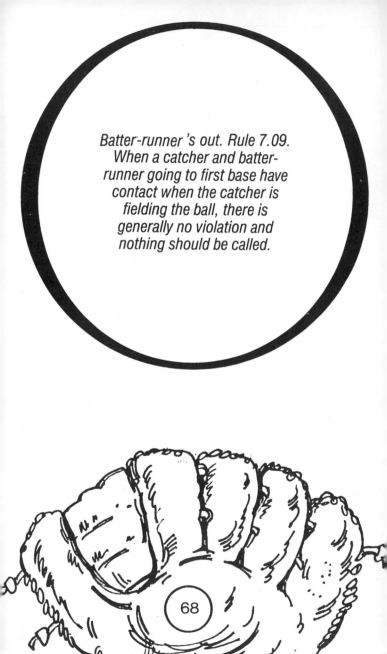

*Batter-runner's out. Rule 7.09.
When a catcher and batter-
runner going to first base have
contact when the catcher is
fielding the ball, there is
generally no violation and
nothing should be called.*

68

Home team starting pitcher in manager's doghouse. Sulking southpaw throws first two pitches of game in the dirt. Seething manager storms out to the mound demanding the ball and very early relief. Animated discussion ensues between manager, pitcher and home plate umpire. Can the pitcher be removed?

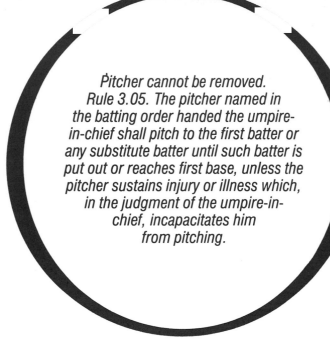

Pitcher cannot be removed.
Rule 3.05. The pitcher named in the batting order handed the umpire-in-chief shall pitch to the first batter or any substitute batter until such batter is put out or reaches first base, unless the pitcher sustains injury or illness which, in the judgment of the umpire-in-chief, incapacitates him from pitching.

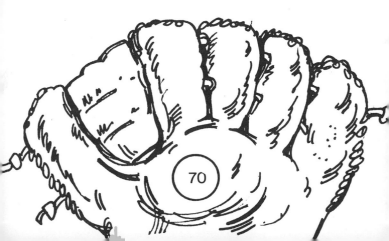

Men on first and third, two out, 2-2 count. Catcher calls for slow curve away, gets ninety-two mile an hour fastball down the pipe. Batter caught looking at strike three, catcher caught looking at ball – lodged in mask. Batter takes off for first, catcher chases, and tags batter halfway up line with ball in mask. What is the call?

Batter is awarded first base.
Rule 5.09. If a pitched ball lodges in the umpire's or catcher's mask or paraphernalia, and remains out of play, on the third strike or fourth ball, then the batter is entitled to first base and all runners advance one base.

72

Man on first, one out. Batter rips drive into right-centre field gap. Runner from first motors around second and flies to third as third base coach windmills him home. Rounding third base, runner out of control crashes into third base coach inside coach's box and renders innocent ancient campaigner unconscious. Runner picks himself up and is caught in run-down between third and home but eventually scores. Does the run count?

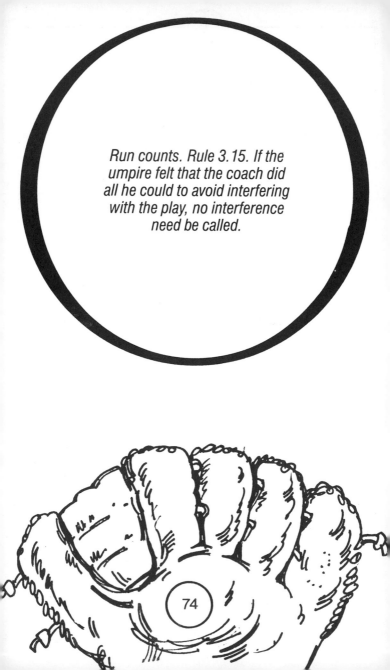

Run counts. Rule 3.15. If the umpire felt that the coach did all he could to avoid interfering with the play, no interference need be called.

Man on third, one out, 0-2 count.
Disregarding runner, pitcher winds up.
Slow runner gets good jump and busts for
home. Called third strike slow curve, and
slow runner arrive at plate together. Ball
deflects off runner at plate and rolls to
backstop. Batter runs down to first.
What is the call?

Batter's out, run scores. Rule 6.05. A batter is out when with two out, a runner on third base, and two strikes on the batter, the runner attempts to steal home base on a legal pitch and the ball touches the runner in the batter's strike zone. The umpire shall call ''Strike Three,'' the batter is out and the run shall not count; before two are out, the umpire shall call ''Strike Three,'' the ball is dead, and the run counts.

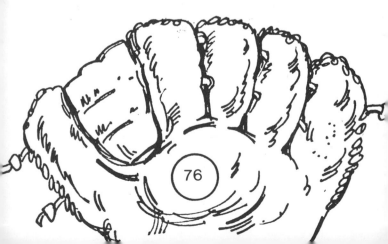

76

Towering drive sends centre fielder back, back, back to the wall. Leaping, acrobatic star goes up, up, up the wall. Perched on top of fence, fielder makes miraculous catch. Unfortunately, force of ball knocks fielder down, down, down off the fence, over the wall, out of the ball park. Home run or fly out?

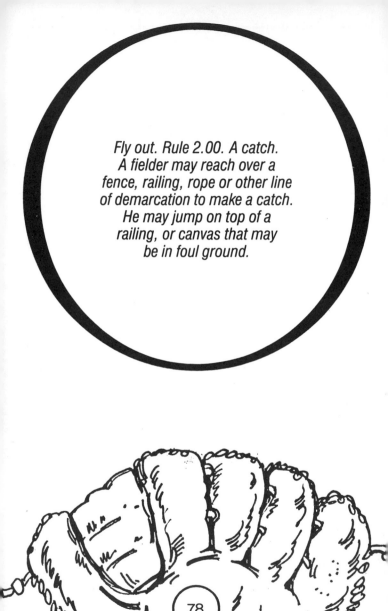

*Fly out. Rule 2.00. A catch.
A fielder may reach over a
fence, railing, rope or other line
of demarcation to make a catch.
He may jump on top of a
railing, or canvas that may
be in foul ground.*

78

Batting order: Little, Small, Petit, Short, Meager. Little singles, Small walks, Short bats in Petit's spot and homers. Meager comes to the plate. Before first pitch to Meager, defensive team makes appeal. What is the call?

Petit is out, runners return to their bases, Short bats again. Rule 6.07. When an improper batter becomes a runner or is put out, and the defensive team appeals to the umpire before the first pitch to the next batter of either team, the umpire shall declare the proper batter out; and nullify any advance or score made because of a ball batted by the improper batter. When the proper batter is called out because he has failed to bat in turn, the next batter shall be the batter whose name follows that of the proper batter thus called out.

80

Men on first and third, nobody out. Batter bunts up first baseline, fair. First baseman hustles in, fields ball on base path, and sets to turn double play. Batter-runner intentionally flattens first baseman. Runner from third scores, runner from first goes to second and batter-runner arrives safely at first. What is the call?

Batter-runner is out, runner from third is out, runner from first base returns to first. Rule 7.09. If, in the judgment of the umpire, a batter-runner wilfully and deliberately interferes with a batted ball or a fielder in the act of fielding a batted ball, with the obvious intent to break up a double play, the ball is dead; the umpire shall call the batter-runner out for interference and shall also call out the runner who had advanced closest to home plate regardless where the double play might have been possible. In no event shall bases be run because of such interference.

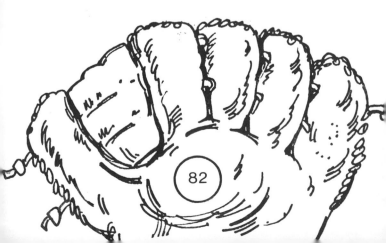

82

Man on third, nobody out. Rocket to left – centre field. Centre fielder and left fielder race for ball with centre fielder getting a piece of drive with top of glove. Juggling act follows with left fielder finally making catch. Runner from third tags when ball is touched and walks across home plate when ball is finally caught. Legal catch, legal run?

Legal catch, legal run. Rule 2.00. A catch is legal if the ball is finally held by any fielder, even though juggled, or held by another fielder before it touches the ground. Runners may leave their bases the instant the first fielder touches the ball

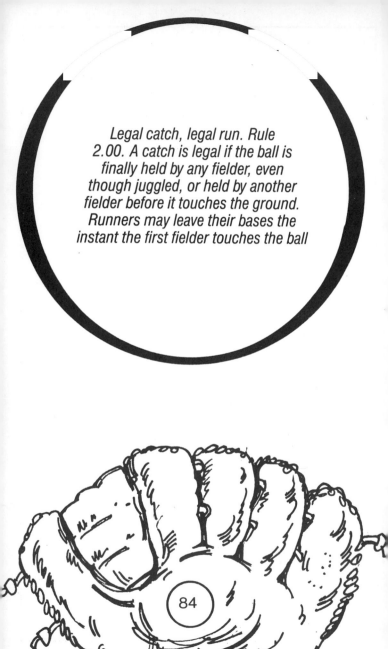

Spit ball specialist given the boot. Next reliever throwing scuffed merchandise. Warned once, classless closer tosses doctored curve for a strike. What is the call?

85

Pitch is a ball, pitcher ejected, and game may be forfeited. Rule 8.02. The pitcher shall not apply a foreign substance of any kind to the ball. PENALTY: For violation of any part of this rule the umpire shall: Call the pitch a ball, warn the pitcher and have announced on the public address system the reason for the action. In the case of a second offense by the same pitcher in the same game, the pitcher shall be disqualified from the game. Rule 4.15. A game may be forfeited to the opposing team when a team, after a warning by the umpire, wilfully and persistently violates any rules of the game.

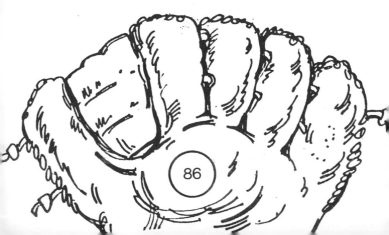

Late season blow-out. Base stealing phenom singles, steals second. Attempting pick-off at second base, pitcher balks. Awarded third base, runner politely but firmly refuses free pass, preferring to take his chances stealing base. What is the call?

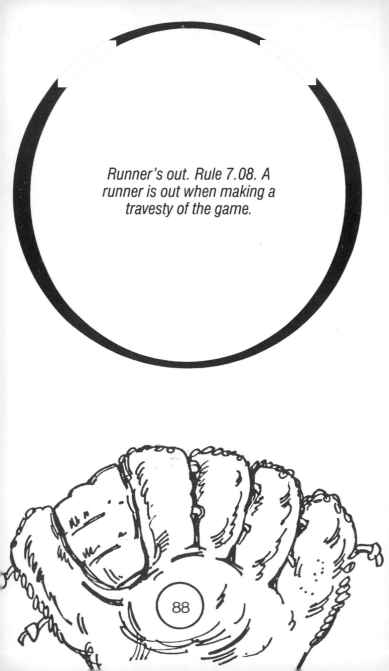

*Runner's out. Rule 7.08. A
runner is out when making a
travesty of the game.*

88

Batter rips line drive up middle. Ball hits edge of pitching rubber and deflects straight towards dugout. Bouncing crazily, ball rolls untouched between first and home and is finally handled by catcher in front of dugout.
Batter-runner stands on first. Single?

Foul ball. Rule 2.00 A batted ball not touched by a fielder, which hits the pitcher's rubber and rebounds into foul territory, between home and first or between home and third base is a foul ball.

90

Bases loaded, one out. Botched squeeze play. Curveball fanned on by batter. Quick catcher up and standing on plate when pitch arrives. Hustling backstop tags out runner from third at plate and then guns down runner from second sliding into third. Double Play?

Balk, runners awarded one base, batter awarded first base.
Rule 7.07. If, with a runner on third base and trying to score by means of a squeeze play or a steal, the catcher or any other fielder steps on, or in front of home base without possession of the ball, or touches the batter or his bat, the pitcher shall be charged with a balk, the batter shall be awarded first base on the interference and the ball is dead.

Power hitter on home run tear. Hot hero steps into fat fastball, bat shatters and out roll the super balls. During ensuing chaos, booed batter makes it safely to first. What is the call?

Batter's out and ejected. Rule 6.06. A batter is out for illegal action when he uses or attempts to use a bat that, in the umpire's judgment, has been altered or tampered with in such a way to improve the distance factor or cause an unusual reaction on the baseball. In addition to being called out, the player shall be ejected from the game and may be subject to additional penalties as determined by his League President.

94

Men on second and third, two out, 3-0 count. Pitcher and catcher working intentional walk, attempt ball four. Outside pitch suddenly clobbered by impatient batter, out of batter's box, standing on home plate. Runners from second and third score. Batter stands on first. What is the call?

Batter's out,
runs do not count. Rule
6.06. A batter is out for illegal
action when he hits a ball with one or
both feet on the ground entirely outside
the batter's box. A batter cannot jump or
step out of the batter's box and hit the ball.

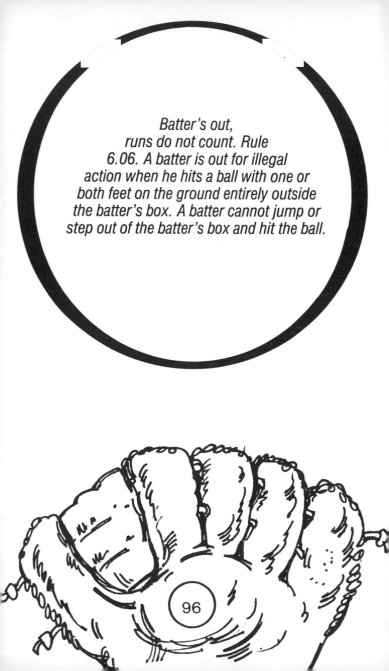

Man on second, two out. Single to centre. Runner from second grazes third base wheeling for home. Scores. Throw from centre field gets by catcher. Batter-runner advances safely to second. Fearing he missed third base and defensive team appeal, runner touches home base and runs back and stands on third. Does the run count?

Run counts,
Rule 5.06. A run legally
scored cannot be nullified by
subsequent action of
the runner.

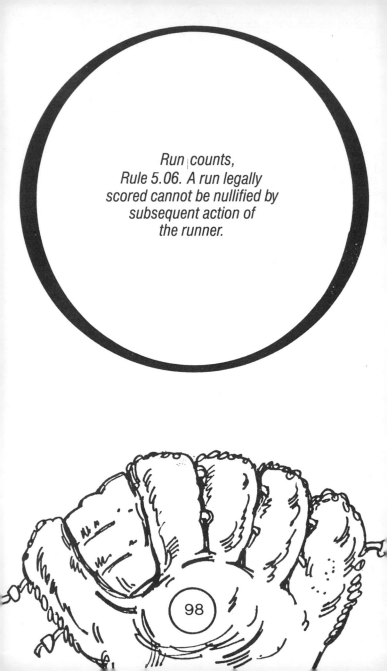

Nobody on, nobody out. Batter pops up
into own dugout. First baseman races into
dugout. Circling under foul pop-up, first
bagger bangs into pitching coach.
Pitching coach, pitching charts,
sunflower seeds, first baseman and ball
all land on floor of dugout.
What is the call?

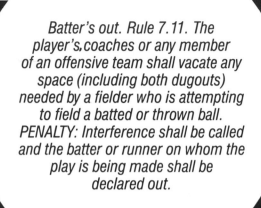

Batter's out. Rule 7.11. The player's, coaches or any member of an offensive team shall vacate any space (including both dugouts) needed by a fielder who is attempting to field a batted or thrown ball. PENALTY: Interference shall be called and the batter or runner on whom the play is being made shall be declared out.

100

Men on first and second, one out. Hot shot one-hopper to error prone shortstop. Inept infielder just waves as ball goes through him untouched and hits runner from second. Ball ricochets into left, the runner from second scores, the runner from first stands on second and the batter-runner stands on first.
What is the call?

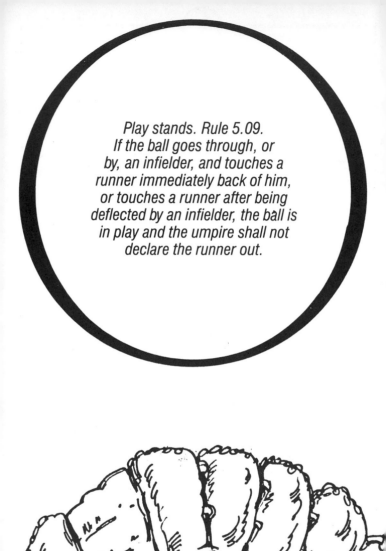

*Play stands. Rule 5.09.
If the ball goes through, or
by, an infielder, and touches a
runner immediately back of him,
or touches a runner after being
deflected by an infielder, the ball is
in play and the umpire shall not
declare the runner out.*

Men on first and second, one out. Lazy, little looper behind third base draws hard charging third baseman, shortstop and left fielder. Runners hold. Catastrophic collision causes players to deflect fly ball into the seats. What is the call?

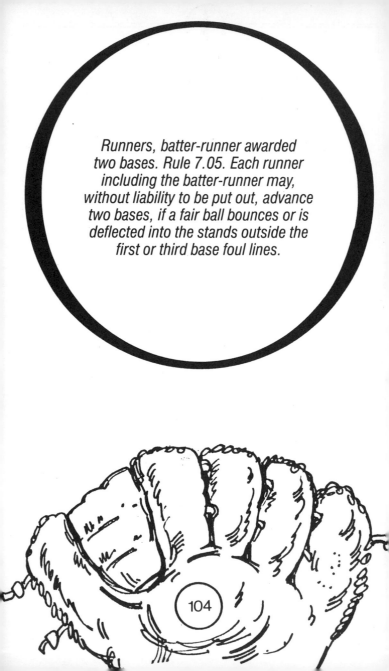

Runners, batter-runner awarded two bases. Rule 7.05. Each runner including the batter-runner may, without liability to be put out, advance two bases, if a fair ball bounces or is deflected into the stands outside the first or third base foul lines.

Men on first and second, two out. Grounder to short. Standing on base path, shortstop gets set to make play but never touches the ball as he is sent flying by runner from second who goes on to score. What is the call?

Runner is out. Rule 7.08. A runner who is adjudged to have hindered a fielder who is attempting to make a play on a batted ball is out whether it was intentional or not.

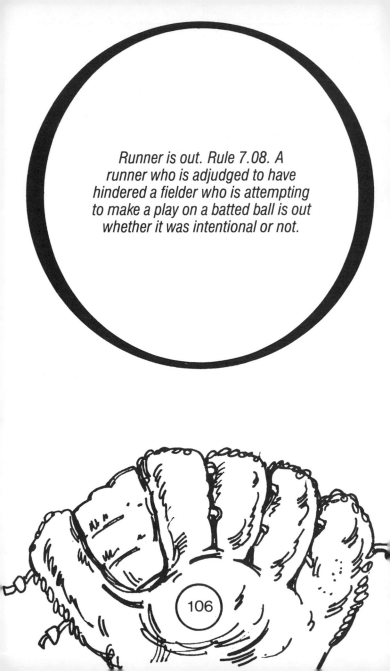

Bases loaded, nobody out. Hot shot to hot corner, fair. Diving third baseman knocks drive down. Prone on base path, fielder corrals escaping ball with his dislodged cap and tags third base for force out. What is the call?

107

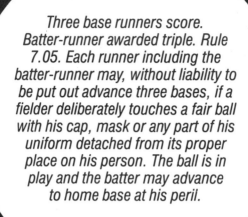

Three base runners score. Batter-runner awarded triple. Rule 7.05. Each runner including the batter-runner may, without liability to be put out advance three bases, if a fielder deliberately touches a fair ball with his cap, mask or any part of his uniform detached from its proper place on his person. The ball is in play and the batter may advance to home base at his peril.

108

Bottom of the twentieth. Tie game.
Visiting team has used complete roster.
Shortstop breaks arm in collision at
second base. Road warriors attempt to
continue contest with eight players.
Legal or illegal?

Illegal, game's over. Rule 4.17. A game shall be forfeited to the opposing team when a team is unable or refuses to put nine players on the field.

Glossary

Appeal *1.* An act by the defensive team to claim a rule violation by the offensive team. *2.* A request by the batter or catcher for the home plate umpire to consult either the first or third base umpire for a ruling on a swing.

Backstop *1.* Catcher. *2.* Wall or fence behind home plate.

Bag Term used for base.

Bang Bang Play Close play at base where thrown or batted ball and runner arrive at base together. Ball bangs glove while foot bangs base.

Batter An offensive player standing in the batter's box.

Batter-runner An offensive player who has finished his time at bat but has not been put out or become a base runner.

Batter's box Marked area within which the batter must stand during his time at bat.

Battery The pitcher and catcher.

Blast A hard hit ball.

Blow-out Lopsided game, one team holding a large lead on the other.

Bombed A pitcher or team that is being beaten badly.

Bottom Last half of an inning, the home teams' at bat.

Bunt Batter taps the ball gently onto the ground close to home plate.

Cleanup hitter The fourth hitter in the batting order.

Closer Relief pitcher who comes in during late innings to end game.

Club *1.* Bat. *2.* Baseball team.

Curveball A pitch that is thrown with an outward twist of the wrist causing the ball to have a sweeping, veering movement as it crosses home plate.

Dead Ball   A ball that leaves the field of play causing a temporary suspension of play.

Diamond   The playing field.

Doctored   A pitched ball that has been illegally tampered with.

Double   Two base hit.

Double Play   Two offensive players are put out by the defense during the same offensive play.

Down the pipe   A pitched ball that travels over the middle of the plate.

Drill   To hit a ball very hard.

Dugout   Area provided for players and coaches to sit, usually located under the stands between home plate and first base and home plate and third base.

Fly ball   A batted ball that goes high in the air.

Fly out   A batted ball that goes high in the air and is caught.

Forfeit   A game ended by the umpire-in-chief in favour of the offended team due to violation of the rules.

Free pass   A play in which an offensive player may advance without being put out.

Gap   the area between the outfielders.

Ground rule double   A fair batted ball that bounces out of the field of play.

Grounder   A batted ball that rolls or bounces close to the ground.

Hanging curve   A curveball that does not move as it crosses home plate.

Hit and run   An offensive play where the base runners advance towards the next base during the pitchers' delivery. Batter attempts to hit ball behind the runners to further advance runners.

Hot corner   Term used to describe third base.

Knuckleball   A pitch that is gripped by the fingertips or knuckles and thrown with no spin on the ball. The ball may move in any direction causing it be very difficult to hit and catch.

Lay one down   Bunt.

Leather   Glove.

Liner   Hard hit ball that travels in a straight line from the bat.

Major League pop-up   A fly ball that stays within the infield but goes extremely high in the air.

Men in blue   The umpiring crew.

Peg   Thrown ball.

Phenom   Excellent young prospect or rookie.

Pop-up   A batted ball that is hit in the air within the infield.

Pickoff   Attempt by the pitcher or catcher to throw to a base to catch a base runner off base for an out.

Pitching Charts   Record of number , location, types and results of pitches thrown.

Protest   A claim by a manager that the umpire has failed to follow the rules.

Pull hitter   A batter who turns on pitches hitting the ball to one side of the diamond. Right handed batters hit to the left side of the diamond. Left handed batters hit to the right side.

Road skipper   Visiting teams' manager.

Road warriors   Visiting team.

Rosin Bag   Bag of resin powder placed beside pitcher's mound. Used by the pitcher to help improve his grip on the ball.

Roster   The players on the team.

Rubber   A rectangular slab of whitened rubber 24 inches by 6 inches, 60 feet 6 inches from the back of home plate. The pitcher must have one foot in contact with the rubber beginning his delivery to the plate.

Run-down   Act of the defensive team to tag out a runner caught between bases.

Single   One base hit.

Spank   To hit the ball hard.

Southpaw   A player who throws with his left hand.

Spear   To catch a batted or thrown ball by diving. To catch a ball by quickly moving the glove.

Speedster   Fast runner.

Tag   A defensive player touches a runner or base with the ball in his bare hand or glove.

Tattooed   A pitcher being hit hard and often by the offensive team.

Triple   Three base hit.

Triple play   Three offensive players are put by the defense during the same play.

Uppercut   An upward swing usually resulting in a fly ball.

Windmill   The waving motion made by a coach or player for a base runner to advance.

Windup   A pitching position where the pitcher faces the batter, holds the ball with both hands in front of his body. With his pivot foot in contact with the rubber, the pitcher may take one step backwards and one forward during his delivery to home plate.

Try to Stump the Ump
Send your questions to
2032 Weston Road Box 114
Weston Ontario Canada
M9N 1X4